Star Girl Saves Fun Day

Jill McDougall

Illustrated by Pedro J Columbo

The children were at school.
They were happy because
it was Fun Day.

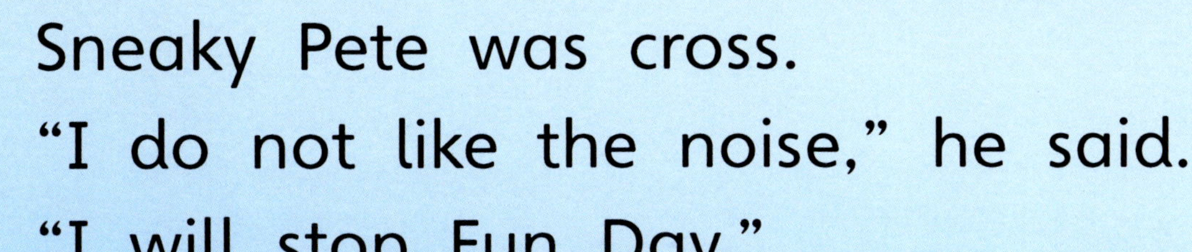

Sneaky Pete was cross.
"I do not like the noise," he said.
"I will stop Fun Day."

"Oh no!" said the children.
"Look at Sneaky Pete!"

Sneaky Pete put foam all over the school.

“That will stop Fun Day”, he said.

"Who will help us?" said the children.
"I will help you!" said Star Girl.

Star Girl flew after Sneaky Pete.

“Oh no!” said Sneaky Pete.
“Star Girl is coming after me!”

Sneaky Pete put foam all over Star Girl.

"That will stop you," he said.
He flew away.

"You cannot stop me," said Star Girl.
She sent out a big net.

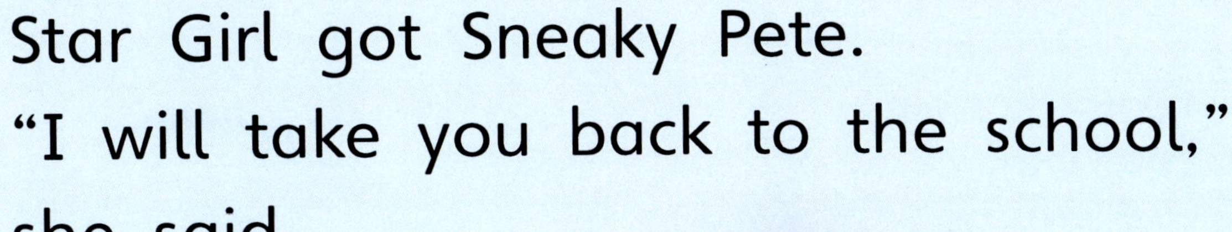
Star Girl got Sneaky Pete.
“I will take you back to the school,” she said.

Star Girl had a plan.
She put the foam on the slide.

The foam made the slide fast.
It was a lot of fun!

Star Girl made Sneaky Pete help, too.
“Thank you, Star Girl!” said the children.